ABOUT THE AUTHOR

Elizabeth Brunoski is a poet, psychologist, and psychoanalyst. She was an English Literature major throughout college, and was the recipient of the Amy Loveman Poetry Award at Barnard College. She went on to complete most of a doctorate in English Literature at NYU. At this point she enrolled in and completed the doctoral program in clinical psychology at the Derner Institute for Advanced Psychological Studies at Adelphi University. Her doctoral thesis was a psychoanalytic biography of the dancer Vaslav Nijinsky. While working as a psychologist she then went to Brooklyn College to work with John Ashbery, eventually completing her MFA in Poetry there. Brunoski also studied with C.K. Williams, William Matthews, and Jane Miller. She received the Himan-Brown Poetry Award from her MFA program. She went on to complete the program at New York University's Postdoctoral Program in Psychotherapy and Psychoanalysis.

Her poems have been published in a number of journals, including *Epoch, Field, Focus,* and *The Normal Review,* as well as an earlier volume, *Crazy Beat* (Terhune Press). Years earlier, in 1969, a play of hers, *Furniture,* was produced at the Side Steps Production Company in Boston.

Brunoski has worked for three decades as a psychotherapist, psychoanalyst, and neuropsychologist, teaching and supervising at several doctoral programs. As a neuropsychologist she specializes in diagnosing and treating learning disorders in children and adults. For two decades she taught a seminar in learning disabilities at Montefiore hospital, and was director of Learning Disability Units at SUNY College of Optometry and Bronx Lebanon Hospital. She also was Director of Training at the Child Study Unit at Postgraduate Center. She lives and practices in Manhattan.

THE
SIDE DOOR
OF THE DREAM

E. J. BRUNOSKI

International Psychoanalytic Books (IPBooks)
New York • http://www.IPBooks.net

Copyright © 2018 E. J. Brunoski

International Psychoanalytic Books (IPBooks),
Queens, NY
Online at: www.IPBooks.net

All rights reserved. This book may not be reproduced, transmitted, or stored in whole or in part by any means, including graphic, electronic, or mechanical without the express permission of the publisher except in the case of brief quotations embodied in critical articles and reviews.

Book design by Dan Williams

ISBN: 978-0-9995965-8-6

for Cliff and Thomas

CONTENTS

1. SNOWFALL.................................... 1
2. TRACES....................................... 3
3. TERMINAL VELOCITY IN CREEPING FLOW......... 6
4. THE LIVE LONG DAY........................... 8
5. IN THE SUNLIT PLAZA......................... 10
6. HOME, POOR HEART, YOU CANNOT REDISCOVER.... 12
7. THE INTERPRETATION OF DREAMS................ 13
8. DISAMBIGUATION.............................. 14
9. TINTYPE..................................... 15
10. TRADING IN FUTURES.......................... 17
11. MILLENIUM................................... 19
12. HORTICULTURE'S LAST STAND................... 20
13. NOT CHOPIN.................................. 22
14. IN THE SLENDER DREAM........................ 23
15. OUT HERE.................................... 24
16. FOXHALLS.................................... 26
17. BE CAREFUL.................................. 28
18. RESCUE...................................... 29
19. IN SIXTH HEAVEN............................. 32
20. SYMPHONY WHILE THE SWANS COME FORWARD...... 34
21. A DISTURBANCE OF MEMORY ON THE ACROPOLIS... 35
22. CHAMBER PIECE............................... 37
23. THAT HAT.................................... 39
24. MY LIFE AS A MEMOIR......................... 40
25. AFTERWARDS.................................. 41

26.	WAKE	43
27.	PLACE	44
28.	ELDRITCH	46
29.	BACK YARD	47
30.	LAST SONG OF THE SERIES	49
31.	ISLAND	51
32.	RIDING FOR A FALL	53
33.	BACK DOOR	54
34.	VIGIL	56
35.	THE SHELLEY SOCIETY	57
36.	ATONAL	58
37.	STILL LIFE WITH SKULL & INKSTAND	59
38.	THE STAIRCASE	60

39.	INTO WORDS	61
40.	IN YOUR ARMS	62
41.	ON A FIFTEENTH-CENTURY FLEMISH ANGEL	64
42.	FOLLOW	65
43.	MYSTERY	66
44.	THE HOUSE	67
45.	1910	69
46.	ACROSS AMERICA	71
47.	LONG HOT SUMMER IN NEWPORT	72
48.	ECHO	74
49.	GIACOMIN'S BIGGEST 0	75
50.	RIGHT ALONG	77
51.	ONE OF A KIND	78

SNOWFALL

Last summer sun showered
into our mornings,
flickering

through heavy green.
We unwrapped
our pale

selves, baring
surfaces
with so much care

you'd have thought
our danger came
from the sky.

Now a blizzard's brightness
settles around us
for miles;

a small wind
in the brush oak;
branches clatter

softly. A world
without memory;
nothing

to hope for
or deny. In sub-zero
clarity

SNOWFALL

our breath
appears
and disappears

and for minutes we love
the pain of speaking.
We hold hands

through goosedown gloves,
in our weightless
camouflage

walk out further into the field
in shifting snow
gathering light.

TRACES

If my shadow left its shape
On the wall, would you know
I had been there? That it was myself
  Who had thrown it there?

No one but me, the lift
Of the hair,
The ginky posture,
My watchful stance,

Then would your shade
Slide forward
To inquire, to show itself
  The two mingling together
So lightly subsuming
Each other.

Etienne de Silhouette,
Minister and Chevalier, in 1769
In his mansion at Bry-sur-Marne
  Preoccupied with his tracings
Cut from black ink on paper,
Vellum, ivory silk, porcelain,

Of faces in noble profile,
Was said to neglect almost everything
Once the act had possessed him

As he sat in the lonely mansion
  So that he himself came to enter

TRACES

Into the stillness of his art,
The shadow from the shadowgraph,
Waiting for it to turn abstract.
Possibly declare itself.

With the advent of the Romantic
Silhouette, the fashionably
Disheveled hair, came the moving
Figures, tripping lightly,
Or kicking up their heels

(Which, if you've tried it,
Is hard to do),
  And children,
With ribboned hats, arms
Linked, a story for each.

I think my shadow
From my shadowgraph

TRACES

Like myself sometimes
  Glides, like myself, is unable
To turn cartwheels
(In fact it has hardly tried),

And what have we thrown
  Together here, to explicate
Our lives? Shouldering

The question, helping whose
Facsimiles to habitate
The hallways
As we sit
In the lovely mansion,
  Jerry-built and brick,
Of traces and our hours,
Absorbed in gesture,

Frontal, sidewise, the stillness
Of our making, adjusting
  Our reflections, together
Entrained in the dance.

TERMINAL VELOCITY IN CREEPING FLOW

It was raining cats and dogs
in the now-friendly dark
not the strangely secret rain
you hardly notice
in a city such as grey
London, such as Seville,
no the downpour
you have to survive
like a childhood that is flame-lit
and shadow-chilled.

Why be so proud
of being lost
when you are after all
traveling at such a speed. And night
does not descend so much as
spin you into the curve
of its arm.

TERMINAL VELOCITY IN CREEPING FLOW

If you are on a ferry
heading toward the mainland
you feel the wind, you cluster
with the passengers.
You might say it can't matter
what you do
when you get there.

A great deed provides
its anticlimax. I honestly thought
I had come in at the end of the party,
and not, as it turned out,
at the beginning.

THE LIVE LONG DAY

On days when I am restless
and questioning, about lost time, I find myself
killing time: the extraneous trip
to the mailbox, news-trawling —
the church murders, the benefits
of butter – then turning back to my employment,
which is helping children understand
the sad side of living.
        The one
unquestionable activity
is a morning walk through Central Park
before the heat arrives. Past Sheep Meadow, down
the allee of American Elms, down
to Bethesda Fountain. Past the settlement
of toddlers, and their minders,
singing "I've been working on the playground
all morning long," to the melody
of "I've been working on the railroad." Past clusters
of preschoolers in orange
summercamp shirts. They will never see one of those
steam locomotives, let alone
work on one.

THE LIVE LONG DAY

     They will probably never hear
the old song
nor understand what it meant
as they age forward
toward spouses, parenthood,
the deaths of their parents.

When I was a young child I liked but never understood
that song, about a rail worker
whose captain shouted to a woman called Dinah,
to blow her dinner-horn for the men. The man also sang,
"Someone's in the kitchen with Dinah,
strumming on an old banjo," and I did not begin
to know what a Dinah meant, what she was doing
about dinner - and about the man
in the kitchen, why it would matter,
why Dinah would even care.

IN THE SUNLIT PLAZA

You may sense
It is about to occur
Gathering its particulars but as yet
      it has no substance

As you turn the corner into two o'clock
It seems you have been waiting for it
But no, it has awaited you.

Here at the pastel bench, along the corridor
Of new-planted beech, is the woman you hoped not to meet
Reducing the distance between you
With an uneven gait. You both have reasons

For her distemper, and one or two more
      to entangle your gaze. This is event is taking
      several wrong turns.

Her lips are voluptuous –
      but that has always caused
      you trouble – arching,
Hypnotic, petal-pale
      but shiny
Her sentences shimmering
      in the air: the harm
Done, the justifications, the harm.

IN THE SUNLIT PLAZA

After, you find your way back
        to the anteroom
Of the Institute. The door reads
PULL; at least you get that right.

When next you meet this memory
It is as a phantom
Decked out with a nimbus, or galloping
Bareback through your sleep, visor
        down so you can't decipher its eyes.

As you step forth to see if it
        finds you familiar
It escapes through
The side door of the dream.

HOME, POOR HEART, YOU CANNOT REDISCOVER

I dreamt you were at the door
in your black wings and hoodie.

But you believe language is gossip. We poled your barge
slowly through the wetlands, through the sawgrass.

Now listen I dedicate two unsettling
anecdotes and an hour's peace of mind.

Your heart is brimming
your head is a bucket of sand.

The room is filling with water,
the room is filling with water and it

is not your dream. Discuss.
Decimal dots are necklaced

like a highway. The two pale birds alight
on the naked shoulder of the tree.

THE INTERPRETATION OF DREAMS

"How pleasant it is to stand in the marketplace,
taking notes on one's neighbor's
behavior."
—Juvenal

Even storks and swallowtails are proven to have dreams.
Egan was only too glad to disentangle
his own thoughts into images.

While they are afloat in the yacht
birds glide past the windows,
matching the speed of the boat so precisely
they can be observed

as clearly as if they were museum displays
hanging on wires.
Still he slept.

Wait a moment, though.
Her raven hair has been compelled into the latest style,
and she is alone in an empty house:

in the garden sheets of aubrietta, in every shade
from lilac to crimson.

Now the birds are back again,

a cold wind is blowing through the park,
then the mist, and the weeping rain.

He has slept in a bed of phantoms.

DISAMBIGUATION

"Being, which is nonsense,
has teeth" (Deleuze). Corollary statements
abound with celerity, like the utility of baize
for aprons and pool tables, which always used to fill you
with apprehension, in those novels. "Body without organs,
body-sieve and glorious body" fail to move the needle
of public opinion wildly in any direction.

This is usually nothing but a face-lifted memory
anyhow, freeing you to proceed
to the lime-green patio. Drinks all around?
Lydia was always so skittish, precocious,
can we get her here, if only for an afternoon?
I don't know why we entertain
circumscriptions of self, such as a profound nickel
allergy overtaking the body, the neck,
the anticubitals - until jetsam lightens

the load. How virid is this valley,
this little one here, sloping to the lake,
where we can mince downward to partake
of true confessions of a fake reality that glimmers
all over, what you do
with what you hear.

TINTYPE

A blur of crinolines on the lawn
of the great house collects the foreground
in this glimpse of Cincinnati,
1897,

the figure urging toward the edge
of the metal plate, as if the perimeter
of that August afternoon could be waltzed across

into alternate arenas, all somehow
more beautiful than the rippling shadows
of the present, the pressure
and stasis in the force field of desire
that one cannot elude

any more than she will eventually elude
my great-great uncle Conrad,
who can dimly be seen poised at the rail
of the porch in a light jacket and a boater,
his eyes, like ours,
on the departing woman.

Later that year, sleeping, they will cross
into the domain of each other's breath;
the next spring she slips
like a vapor
from the ongoing albums.

TINTYPE

You can almost make out
the pretty face. As she imprints
a sidelong glance at the photographer,
is she declaring (as a subject declares)
her half-held foreknowledge, and a willingness
to proceed with her uncertain role
in the narrative? Her slight form

is tilted, tensed: no, she is too rapt
to comment. I think
she is signalling how this moment
is a whispered phrase,
the stain of light that drenches it
into memory allowing her her only postponement,

as she hurries her irreversible
transparency now
home, now away from home, stage left, her tiny
pointing foot seeming to near
the metal edge, at last, the mercy
and containment of your palm.

TRADING IN FUTURES

That was not an emblematic dream. You were wrapped
in a little jacket with its silk-lined pockets.
A name was scribbled hastily on paper.
You sensed the progression that webs
into your most wakeful hours: your wild
way of reading. The place

is a viney place. Here
we are at the corner, as always: wafting
to a kind of rest. The streetlight
crackles. Someone's dwarf has come
to find you. Now the aptness of the darkening
street to designate a lifetime
of proliferating conclusions is lost, lost

in your arrival at the larch-held yard,
the house with its beckoning
archways and parlors, the impulsive
staircase allowing you access
to a boxful of memories you thought
were never permitted in photographs. You sort
through those you can. But nothing is profane
anymore, here where your dew-drenched
excursions are unintended,

unattended offerings. Even your fallen
brother, who suddenly approaches
on the sidewalk, is absorbed into the fabric
of his inquiry. Years collapse into his smile,
which is itself. Why ever should he have
to die? You breathe, this dream
breathes, in its wholehearted
flexibility: a voluminous car containing the sun

and everything under it. Then after the gibberish
of early morning waking, the sturdy
animal that leads you into
your life. Which, if you've noticed, lately grows
more secular, and furnished.

MILLENIUM

What smile is it that is still
So secret we would travel anywhere now
In our minds to find it

The parcel arrives
Just at the moment dew
Forms in your latitude: a long
Trumpet call that brings us indoors

To discover the face of the quarrel
In the music room is tearstained
And is fair, but we have not won
Its intimate favors. If only there were
More privacy. Yet pilgrims never leave
The doorway; once they arrive

Their remaining is as firm
As their journey.
Those of us who have found
Our reflections, why shouldn't we
Begin to mention the rooms
Of violence, where we lost

Our good sense. And it is years we wish
To recover; as we sleepwalk
Into the millennium
And we are widely instructed

In the very freedom to fish and forage
Once more with our hands
Alert, like paws, even when it is only water
We catch, we catch it so flawlessly.

HORTICULTURE'S LAST STAND

All those cadillacs and motorcycles: sullen
ornamental plants. Or another
way: the antique postcard as an echo
of the present; the word-perfect actor dying of hunger
for reality in the face of the audience's
explicit joy.

The necessary ratio
of genius to common sense is
a cryptograph of magisterial simplicity
and forbearance. The wild growth
of the larger view emended by the years we are
an idiot savant at love. Remember,

in every seeming
coincidence there are two things
you should remember:

how our minds,
in their meticulous candor, persist
in enjoying murdering
Marilyn Monroe. Two, you are bound
by the spurious departures to eat
off a promissory timetable.
The lilacs come back to us

HORTICULTURE'S LAST STAND

with the sincerity of the early days
of television.
And the stylish idea
of the diary as confidant was our last unquoted
folie-a-deux,

our unquoted assumption that as you are reading this
you are becoming
gradually undesirable,
that is to say, indecipherable, to the future.

NOT CHOPIN

The lake was quiet.
The mirrors in the oak frames had certainly been polished.
There was no one around anywhere.

Annan was startled to read his own name in the visitors' book.
He had never contemplated the moral value of actions.
After last night there was no turning back.

A fat marble nymph crouched on the veranda.
Annan had a terrible memory for faces.

Maybe her letter would simplify everything:
He reconciled himself to waiting, or to its opposite.
China had never seemed so near.

Even the weary need a rest.
Out on the terrace he stood and surveyed:

All the glittering half-emptied glasses.
The one red scarf on the lawn.

IN THE SLENDER DREAM

The water is barely lapping across
the slats of the pier, lapping at its farthest reach
into the lake.

I thought of
Bitcoins in a petri dish, also the small mosses,
and surely embryos. We labor to create.

You tell me these elbow-length gloves
are still employed by falconers. Of Devon,
of Devonshire
of Riverside Park.
The wind is coming,
surely.

We pass through the lychgate
to the little churchyard where I can ask my father
whether my father is here because I see him
at such a distance. It is peaceful in the forest.
Why don't we remain here?
Place your feet on a bed of leaves.

There is a line of women
returning home at the end of the day.

We are moving again, almost running,
almost breathless. We have to get there,
just off the beach before the last slats
disappear

OUT HERE

I could always see dust motes
in the sunbeams at three o'clock, but now
I also see angels. Perhaps this
means maturity. Tonight you and I will go out
to lure the eclipse we have traveled
so long for with such lenses and hope;
we need a sign because it is no longer enough

to have babies and give them
the names of streets and flowers.
Our problem is memories
we can't touch with our fingers.

In the same way, at pitch-midnight, we think
our dreams will slow down
for repairs – but the dumbwaiter rises,
see! with parts of the body on a tray.
We have always only seconds
to find just the right thing to do
though you are always with me
in the dark and I trust you
the absolute way I would trust my golden

OUT HERE

retriever if I had one, a soft and invincible
one that the children use as a pillow,
that sleeps at our feet soundlessly, and passes
on with the leaves in November (we can't
discuss why). Though now we look up to find
the Dog Star was left as a channel-marker
at a tilt for others equally exploring
in the night sky. Like grownups

entering rooms where they suddenly
are not wanted, we feel both far
away and more physically real
than we expected, but where it is
so sandy, and without banishment,
out here, where now infinitely

softly a giant
sits down on the horizon
like the solid limits of our minds.

FOXHALLS

I've lived in New York City all my adult life
and I will probably die here, although most days I still
only half believe that, or a little more than half
by now, the years inch by. Before that I lived nearby
in New Jersey, with a large back yard with cherry trees
and robins that ate the cherries, although my father
tried to prevent them, using nets.

                Behind the yard was an old estate
of over eighty acres, and a vast, I thought, main house
that went untenanted most of the year. Or perhaps
one person lived in it, caretaking perhaps, but you never saw
anyone, or even a car driving up to it, during the day.

                                This was called
Foxhall Territory, and all of us in the neighborhood
used it as our playland. We swung on the vines that grew tangled
downward from the overgrown elms, and we were Tarzans,
and later some of the boys were in a jungle war. When Disney's
Robin Hood came out, we were archers, making our bows and arrows
using string and the pliable branches from the ten-foot beech
hedgerow that enclosed the property, until one day my father
came out and shot one of the arrows vertically into the air,
and when it went up about fifteen feet he took away the bows
and arrows.

                    We used to enter the property through a little opening
we had made in the hedge. No one
ever dared to go up to the front door of the mansion
because on good authority we had learned it had a ghost.
Once my brother nearly made it, but he turned back.

FOXHALLS

                         After I moved
to New York to go to college I heard that Foxhalls as we called it
had been turned into condominiums. The name
lingered, for me, so I researched and found one Thomas Foxhall,
from London, had owned the property and in 1927 was accused
of murdering a young woman in his employ. An unusual case
because the woman was educated and because she was murdered
in Manhattan, on East 29th Street, so the court proceedings
took place in New York.

                       I could not find the outcome of the trial. When I told
my sister what I had solved out she said she wasn't
so sure, she herself had seen a ghost in the 18th-century section
of her current home, and at present that's how the matter stands.

BE CAREFUL

An afternoon can carry you up
Like a small child on the shoulders of a crowd
Waiting along the canopy to be included for a moment
In the entourage of the famous person

Who arrives looking not at all
Like his photographs. Oh, you know this.
And yet you obey traces of expectation
That seem to belong to you, not the others.

You suddenly want to go back to the crater lake,
Where you were happy, or rush to explain
Why there are so many black cars. And then
Where you are going becomes tangled in your fight

To think of one thing as simple as a room.
In your childhood, the magician's wand,
An infinite straight line, could be divided
Into segments, each also a straight line,

But when you dropped them, they sprung arms
Like starfish. Be careful! He said, Careful!
He stooped and collected them into the hat, where
The oysters were completing their pearls.

RESCUE

On an afternoon no better
than others, a sharp
wind dusting snow off the drifts, they bundled
into their down, crossed with scarves, and started
across the lake from school, he after decimals
and the Civil War, his sister coming from the sounds
and sights of the alphabet, the middle letters,
harder to remember, so she called them out for him,
tired and exacting, with each third step, the plosives
extending her breath importantly
until she spotted the boat house and the black
spruce, and stopped, looking
to her side, where there was
no one, then to the other, then around
to where he was struggling carefully
from a break in the ice to lift
and lever his body back onto the surface
but losing strength in the pull
of the current.

      Someone called out
and the older children, and now grownups made
a lifeline with their bodies
and clothing, but were pressing new
fissures toward the opening. They were
an experienced couple, so she started
to work in from the side, knowing very well how
his body was heavy enough to support
her weight, which would just do to crawl across
this ice pushing the long branch that he
could grasp, she hold, and she bared

RESCUE

her hands to hold his and to work their way
slowly along the branch back
outward, to the reach of the neighbors
who now solemnly or tearfully vied
to receive him with blankets
and their questions, could he move his legs just
nod, and, how could a child so young have known
to save a child.

      Shuddering, seeking out
faces, he could hardly describe
how he had been frightened but not surprised
to see her crawling and sliding
closer, their gazes steady, as if they
would discuss this now. In fact, she
could tell them - but now she was gone: back,
it seemed, to find her gloves, and hearing

this, he was first, half-lumbering, knowing
the way, so as she disappeared he just dove
beneath the surface to find her, and whether
he could find her they would have to wait to know.

She stood at the back of the kitchen,
listening to the unfamiliar figure
at the doorway announce his news in a steady,
low voice. Before it settled
into her, before she moved, collecting dry
clothing, and hurried and stumbled to join the gathering
vigil at the lake, she half attended, half

RESCUE

reminded herself to teach them
better, now, to tell a cold wind
from the beginnings of a thaw. It occurred
that if she had not taught them
so well to mind each other, then one
would still be left. But which one?
How effortlessly
they had opened her life at its center
to guide her into questions she had never felt
as her own. Later, gazing
into the dark window in the ice, she tried
to surmise how those we tend can pull us, willing,
into any infinity. She could already make out
the beginnings of dreams that would become
no less real than other memories:
        At first, she calls
and calls in a large, bright room. Then their figures
float with her in a shadowy
liquid, their hands reaching for her - as no doubt
they had - and they are swimming hand-in-hand, searching
less for the original opening
than a use for this knowledge
of traveling beyond borders, where loss
becomes never larger or smaller,
but only proceeds in time,
surfaces are divisions of our own making, like
waking, a child, a voice.

IN SIXTH HEAVEN

You are wearing sandals, your hair back
loose, and slightly too-textured clothes,
but so is everyone else. You have been handed

a set of instructions, in the form of a myth
from your birthland, in blank verse, with a sudden drop
toward a normal life for the hero,

which brings you to tears. You must now choose
whether, for your remaining space, you wish to be loved
or misunderstood, and whether for your body,

your prize-winning life, or your private questioning
smiles. At the same time,
for your improvement you may pencil in

the faces of persons familiar enough
to be thought of as goals, in the sense
of frame houses as livable

goals, with pictures on the walls
of vaguely sinister cousins, who are invited anyway
for the holidays. The hero has won

his recognition, though it doesn't look like much
more than his rote pose and grimaces
accumulating in his shaving mirror over hundreds

IN SIXTH HEAVEN

of days. Is this how
he has eliminated from his life
extremes of handsomeness, humdrum evil, hero-

worship of himself, that march toward endless
speculation on improved color combinations,
verbal murders, all the primary gunk

of late afternoons? Here is a life-sized question.
This is heaven. Everyone is moving slowly
around you, but at a constant rate,

so it feels only like time passing. If you
are able to recite the ending to the story
without a twinge of revision, name the hero's

three grown children, and the recipe he finally
chokes on, you may go on to the airport,
where over the loudspeaker you should try

to pick out a proper noun that is a code name
for your name, but not yet for you.
Your lift will take you

to your last heaven, which is immaculately
the same.

SYMPHONY WHILE THE SWANS COME FORWARD

— After Henry Purcell

The countertenor wants a kiss,
   but the violist is unsure.
It has been this way for some while.
Without the uncertainly of mirrors
   & the mirroring still waters of ponds.

Watchful into dusk is the other
   pair of eyes, rimmed
In black, as eyes then seldom were.

The Queen does not let herself remember
How she is always surprised by the approach
   of darkness. She thinks
How the mating of these players
By couples, or trebles, is so needed
   & so undefined.

She sends to war her hero
   as though she knew nothing of violence.
Within the year she is suddenly dead.

It is the seventeenth century. Night
   herself is here.
Slowly & without irony
   the masquers defile among the trees.

A DISTURBANCE OF MEMORY ON THE ACROPOLIS

He had never seen so much sunlight.
It seemed all unreal, this apparition
from his schoolbooks; at the same time
too real, a lively sea-serpent
that makes one wonder,
when it surfaces, Why didn't I
believe it more?

Wishing is cheap, Freud
wrote, a ragged stand-in
for the palpable present. But lately, the world
was moving too fast, too fast. He slept little,
and badly. He scarcely had time to dream.
                                      Bicycles

distressed him, and railway cars reminded
him of traveling to Bern
with his mother, who stripped half-naked
in the compartment at night. Still,
Vienna was lonely

and ungrateful. Was here,
at last, a father
he could not annihilate,
a goddess he could come to
not as an urchin, insistent, but as
that most absurd of suitors,
a sensible grown man? How beautiful

A DISTURBANCE OF MEMORY ON THE ACROPOLIS

were these chiseled
shadows, so different from the monotone
grey of Berggasse! Would the voices
of these remains speak to him
secrets he had always known, but wanted
to hear aloud - like the gossiping stones
of Ilios, to their dear
discoverer? In the soft wind

he thought of his sister Anna
at the keyboard (was it possible
he could remember?), the silvered
larkspur on the teacup he flung
at her to keep her
from practicing. Yes, it was rational

foolishness: he had always believed that all
the Greek world was a lullaby
sung to another, and healthier,
progeny. Now they listened: the caryatids,
fixed in their loveliness,
the Ionic pillars, gently

swollen at the base
to make them appear perfectly straight,
like the wavering straight
line of earliest
desire, this
impossibly blue sky, and
Ich bin dein -
- I am yours -
he said.

CHAMBER PIECE

From our first moment
we have wanted to touch.
But look
at our lives (we have meant to say): so windingly
alien in their textures, their hues,

though their subjects
run willingly side by side, holding hands at the end
of a giddy, infinite perspective (one arguably, perhaps,
with spires? With cloudy vast
allowances?) But all we can see
is the organizing dot
on the horizon where the world seems to fall off

into the fresh air
of nothing at all: calling and calling us
to no place like home.

The experienced sky
has so often helped: with its clear
own mind, its beglamored recklessness
that can veer us to a remove
whose assured shadows
devour ambiguity.
The weather points from the gift
of its face to the careless indoors
we wish to contain: white walls strung
with archways of discussion
and assent. By the time we have found our way back
to the anteroom of particulars,

CHAMBER PIECE

the exquisite vase of the afternoon
will be overturned, our words encoding the advances
of dusk, along the challenge
of the bright
spilled petals, on the surfaces
where the petals lie.

THAT HAT

I did not spend $900 on a hat.

Not a hat by Nick Fouquet, hatter
to Madonna, Gigi Hadid,
to Bob Dylan and Sia. Who can put fifty feathers

on a brim and make it work
in a low-key continental surfer
sort of way.

I do not speak about things that are not true.
Because I think that becomes exigent.

I would like to insist that you come with me
to the vast ranges of the Southwest
where rolling new choices are possible
because of the solitude.

I do not like to hide, I do not like
to be found. Though perhaps you do, I will
count on you to tell me.

Please leave your sandals, and your dry cleaning,
by the door when you come in.

I used to like Brooklyn.
One of those hats has copper medallions
all across the hatband!

And, I am not writing this poem.

MY LIFE AS A MEMOIR

The auspicious morning has begun.
The vinyl 78 spins out Khachaturian's "Sabre Dance."

The animal in your arms has turned
into a metaphor, a fast-metasticizing omen,

but for what exactly? We stood together, the light jinking
off fragments of mica on the ground.

You were patient. I was on the bus
crosstown, to the grassy edge of the river (but which river).

We stood right on the water. Later we arrived
in the darkened square off Astor Place,

not that you'd call that any kind of destination.
But anyhow we were all a young kid.

And we know this well. The ocean's reach
nearly claims the giggly toddler. A sole candle

almost lights the curtain in flames.
This alley is a cinema, a black road of images

where somewhere a heroine is fleeing
the unspeakable danger in her stiletto heels.

AFTERWARDS

> *"There is something that goes in the direction
> from the past to the future..."*
> —Jean Laplanche
> psychoanalyst and winemaker

Alma saw the garden with high brick walls.
Most of it seemed to be paved with square, round,

and pentagonal beds in which dwarf conifers made a green
contact with the brown winter twigs

of what she imagined were flowering shrubs. The walls were covered
with neatly trimmed fruit trees. There were snowdrops

in bloom. Here and there, the stark
spreading roots of a climbing jasmine. The grey stone hare

peered from a bed of eranthis. The end wall
was pierced by a really beautiful pair

of wrought iron gates, leading to a second
walled garden beyond.

This doctor had tried to explain that an outrage,
or a flourishing, could be felt for the first time

AFTERWARDS

in distant years: the implantation
of the enigmatic message. Afterwardsness
he called it.   Sometime later

she would know where to follow. Everything
should be made as simple as possible.

She was to discover there were four
of these gardens, one behind

the other, each larger, and less
formal than the last.

WAKE

Wake quickly
and save what you can.

The water is at your window,
just the opaque blue-black you'd always expected.

You are in the eye of a storm that waits
and watches but does not harm you.

Hurry with your clock and photos,
hurry with your best friend.

Your room with its walls cannot help you,
and your half-finished dream

is a boat too big for the doorway.
Take up your name, and swim.

PLACE

It says here in the Science Times that ghosts
are the ultimate agoraphobics, they have an extreme
attachment to a space, and can't let go. I don't know
how anyone would know that, since it seems to me
that ghosts have already departed

to quite a distance, but then perhaps
perception is everything, and I have never
actually seen a ghost, have you?
   Are you
one of the selected ones, abashed and thrilled
to perceive the departed, the having-gone-so-far-
but-that's-far-enough: suddenly, in the corner
of your bedroom, out in your back yard,
milling around or wafting
lugubriously.   Lingering to their place.

   Frances Glessner Lee, heiress
turned criminologist, made dollhouse dioramas
of unexplained murder scenes,
meticulously, lovingly, domestic death
squinched into a nutshell, and for her good works was made
an honorary Police Captain in Baltimore, in 1943,

the first woman in the U.S. to hold that rank.

PLACE

You may still view them if you wish,
or, you might not wish. She said that she had felt captive
until her brother died, and she
was freed to pursue a vocation.

   Glessner Lee helped solve cold cases by minute
attention to detail: the stove door left open, the tiny
blood spot on the window sill.
Eventually it became clear to those who felt
they were able to know

that her dioramas were tenanted
by the original victims,
who could occasionally be seen

settled into the thimble-sized
drawing rooms and kitchens, having arrived
at the necessary harbor to stand in
for the familiar bloodied
havens from which they had been torn.

ELDRITCH

From the other side of the rustic
   door they heard a small voice
pleading for some verses. The old
   woman, tears rising,
made for the kettle. She met
her sister's protest.

"It's only a child, hungry, maybe
   homeless." But "No, no no,"
her sister cried, "it is the eldritch
   that eats ends of poems – that
distracts you then out of your very
grasp snatches   the

BACK YARD

Don't you wish your life
could be revised,
edited, rejiggered,
sent back

But how do you enter the point
of turning, and how would you know
what to wish for?

When I was eleven
I grew a plot of tomatoes and herbs,
peppermint and rosemary, that astonished me
because of how lavishly they grew
and fed the neighborhood

because in fact they mostly grew
by themselves so I branched out to lettuce
and that is when I found out
we had rabbits.

What I would do instead now
what I would change now
is to go downstairs at night,
down the impossible dark house
down through the house
and what I know is lurking there
waiting for me there

BACK YARD

and go out to the garden
I had planted, to watch
in little moonlight, the rabbit
I knew would be there

munching the rows of lettuce.
I would sit there,
it would be there

in the mystifying
person-free darkness
the two of us
watching in the dark.

LAST SONG OF THE SERIES

As you always expected: God – himself - comes to you
in his metal wings, and you feel
the chill. Which interlude,
even in waking,
does not prevent the legend,
and others, from continuing to stalk you
as they will.
Should I be afraid?
you want to ask;
Will you still help me?

In the face
of these visitations
your personal awareness finally
is - whose? Or will it at last evaporate
into its origins, cancel
until it solves perfectly
into zero:
bliss.

An unalterable
longing is the final stage
of the progression, as well
as being the first, outshining the hand-hewn
prisms of attainment. And at times

our happily threadbare surfaces
lead us through the ranges
of something entirely surmised,
to free us from the revolving door
of our leave-takings, and the half-assurance
of their incompletion.

LAST SONG OF THE SERIES

The impossible request is
Go
from my window;
and the veils
alluded to in the last song
of the series were mine, all mine,
tattered insistently
into whispers, perplexed and diminishing
as the trellis that lifts them, gently and firmly upward
into the expanding cuff of time.

ISLAND

When you come home I can help with the child.
There are weeks of questions to undergo,
We'll ask the neighbors to help with preparations.
On Sunday morning after the birds calm down
We can walk the length of Manhattan Island
And arrive at a plaza where we locate our mystery.

With so much to think about it is hardly a mystery
That we want to spend some time in peace, free as a child
Left sunning on some pleasant desert island
All morning and afternoon with nowhere to go
Until the tide comes in and the sun goes down
And it grows time for adoration.

But we must be careful if we plan a next evasion
Even if we have to go far and invent a mystery
And a newer place for us to search around
Where we would like to stop being childish
Instead of batting around in the dinghy to and fro
And wishing we could arrive at an entirely new land.

That is the whole purpose of an island.
Where the happy hordes all stand in veneration.
If you have ideas you should let me know.
One of the urgent needs is to dismantle the mystery
And wherever it leaves me, to help the child
And sing it to sleep at night and put it down.

ISLAND

This will work beautifully. We will go down
And take off from the middle of the island
To see if we can locate some wilderness,
It's not like this is a linear equation.
And we could waft on a real dose of mystery
There are so many questions to undergo.

If we are not bested by the undertow
If we can make it there instead of drowning
Perhaps it's a way to reconfigure the mystery.
This time I would prefer to live on high land.
As a kind of permutation.
If you're not home I can help with the child.

This can be our reparation on the island.
We can finally batter down the mystery.
Wherever you go I will help the child.

RIDING FOR A FALL

can be the opening advantage
at the roadhouse where Trailways pays the audience
to weep. The rest is dimly
negotiable. It is possible to betray everyone
at once.

More nomads skid up on the gravel, in the cocksure way
their women will miss them, or pull their names
out of bed at this hour, even just for the publicity.
By eleven, most
have removed their hats, but have forgotten how to
   surface.
Reinforcements
are sent for, real amphibians starting up from the murky
midtown tunnels,

because the guys need a little encouragement,
their lives are so short and effortless.
You remember
that code of ethics: it used to be scary, but clean.

BACK DOOR

We lie in front of the fire
In each other's arms:
Animals homing to light and heat.
Like a door
The fire opens
And we are standing alone
Again, fully clothed
In our corduroys for autumn.
The streets do not
Have names, but we know
Who lives in the houses.
Our names are being called
By someone's female relative
Which means that the day
Is ending.

Somehow we have to
Get inside. I try
A back door, afraid
You are looking

BACK DOOR

For me in another home
Where I will never find you.
You are no longer
Powerful enough
To know where I am. The streets
Grow longer. Suddenly I am aware
You are forgetting my face
In a stranger's living room,
You are so frightened;
Soon I will slip from your memory
Entirely and vanish
From the world.

The only way
To make this bearable
Is to realize
we are dreaming,
we will - yes - wake now,
touch each other's
face, not fall from each other again.

VIGIL

the war flickers
& grows cold

no one will come
here now

when the rains let up
we have a kind
of vigil

candles lit
at noon

photos of the
mud huts

every name
hidden

in hands
cupped
at our dark tables

THE SHELLEY SOCIETY

—for William Matthews

Today the Shelley Society
was missing

at the fairground
where you painted faces.

We checked
several times,

we searched
the booths.

There was only a pensive
young woman on a rock.

But was she
the Shelley Society?

ATONAL

Possession

in what measure?

                      fire

that crosses
morning

wind

        racking
        the orbit

                like fire

in a small box

STILL LIFE WITH SKULL & INKSTAND

It's a scholar's
desk, despite
the butts
& gin reek

iron lamp
inkstand
of malachite

centuries
steep
in the vellum

he lives
alone, calls
this home

blackletter & bone

THE STAIRCASE

This is the staircase that Rudolph Valentino
used to steal up to visit the woman
he loved, leaving horse and driver to wait
the whole night, in the days when sheep grazed
Sheep Meadow. His ghost, with its signature hat,
was later seen in the hallway, knocking and knocking
at a door. Now I slip down
the staircase to save time, or to not be seen
on certain days, or I study the cadmium blue
veins of the marble as I trudge up, slowing,
with groceries and books.

      On the top floors I love
how the branching sconces cast archways of shadows
along the halls. On clear nights there, we open
the door to a roofscape of treetops and stars.
Somewhere in the building are two cellists.
Once, on the second floor I met a woman sitting
with her face in her hands. Sometimes the journalist
stops to make conversation and discreet verbal
advances. I haven't told you this.

      When I told you
about the ghost, your laugh was a question
and its reply. You jog over through the park
in your weatherproof jacket, pause to take
the elevator, enter with your key.

INTO WORDS

So that even our gestures had grown
organic, tendrils and tassels of the early
spring, hardly begun but articulate;
you could imagine them

already broadening, extending into the woven bowl
we had become together. There is a song
that mentions this. Somewhere in Ohio a tall blond singer

holds the larger pattern up to view. At this distance
our actions can be gracefully
explained, and we grow to love the explainer
who trellises our privacy. Last summer we loved

the small towns we traveled through
trying out houses we imagined
we could live in, like local ghosts flickering across
the embracing porches. We arrived in town,

and arrived in town. Every morning
our dreams collapsed in slow motion, our touch
redefining home. Now each practical act

could recede into its token, the way widows-walks
eventually appeared on inland roofs,
on Broadway, filigree enclosures
where the mind can pace, reorganizing some idea
of watery departure.

IN YOUR ARMS

I see it now: home is where we come to wing down
or are routinely sent to be lost
and rediscovered in extreme
consummation: this openness
to everything - color, words, unnameable objects
and propositions - or this chancing it
to be routed into the monotonous glory
of a pale circle of insight
as it enters our lives with a mystifying shock.

Or home can be a designation
that applies to the action of never coming home,
setting out through fields of strange sweet gold
scattered with way stations
of abandon (your name enters
the picture increasingly
sharply).

In our days along the river, before the highways
were put in, there were those houseboats
sucking at the banks, and real gypsies
living on the visibly seeping hulls, and I
was drawn to this defiant uselessness.
On nights filled with the moans
of tugboats, I also wanted
to slip off from the embankment
of embrace (I'm sorry), with one of those absurdly colorful
bandannas wound tightly around my sensible reserve
and into evidence that a future,
not just ardent leanings,
ever, anywhere, took place. To sleep with something wild
under unfathomable changes
of design was an abeyance that stretched itself

IN YOUR ARMS

into the far reaches of definition:
of the dark or lambent taken-for-granted
"us" of those days. I was alone with my impatience

in that it seemed so beautiful. We both thought so.
We wondered then how we could lose our ways,
even our understanding of them,
because in our time and place everything is so
talked about, worried into words
as if personal privacy were an openness
into oneself impossible to achieve again.

But here, we have restored some place:
it is so quiet here,
neither obscure nor bright,
and I am grateful
for your silence, our cradling
arc of desire; how it is amply remote, like a rainbow
that we point to and that protects us,
as we find ourselves alighting
slowly at the center
of things, with tomes of gesture opening the way leaves
flutter without direction in the wind.

ON A FIFTEENTH-CENTURY FLEMISH ANGEL

At once there is
The messenger.
In broad-winged
Dignity, his finger poised
Against the air, a gesture
Of benevolence.

    But closer,
One can make out a flush
Of color up his cheeks,
As if he took a sly sport
In quitting airy vigil
To touch his toes
Against the earth.

    And upward
Through the portico
The tiny, steepled
Landscape is no distant
Visionary whim: armies setting out
Through fields strewn
With lovers in the sunlight.

FOLLOW

It doesn't matter how much dismay
you feel, it doesn't matter how much high-
concept Eurotrash staging, your stingy-
brim fedoras, it is all the guttering-candle

glow of an already fading age
in acres of cozy, frowsy gardens.
Did you know that "clan"

means simply "children"?
What if one were no one's child.

You were in a foreign, a very foreign place
chasing the thought of a woman gone before you,
you were not ready for her
to leave you had this question, and almost,
you could almost

see her again, the whippet eyes, the dripping
lilacs, comes this thought, this image-
thought, this signifier baffling
in its simplicity, and you heard it

calling, "Follow me, follow me,"
harder and faster than anyone
had reason to hope.

MYSTERY

Mystery surrounds massive garbage pile in Pacific.
Sotomayor sworn in as nation's first Hispanic Justice.
"Talent" hopeful mortifies judges.
Tomorrow's weather will be cloudlessly sane.

Despite his status as a digital native, the organist played
a dirge as sad as the wind in a ruined window. I find
from my enneagram that I am more a Loyalist
than an Investigator, that is, engaging, responsible,
anxious, and suspicious. This was in my prayers?

Aren't you always excited
about the new discoveries at Stonehenge,
the sister henges, the idea of a whole nested
community bustling around
all those un-ironic megaliths.

THE HOUSE

The only furniture left
was the pythons. "But you never stay long,"
said Mother. "Come in. The house is selling."

Whee, I thought, no more dust bills,
no waiting up for the moaning spectre.
"Here." I brought the paper,
the oral report, and some familiar animals
to fry. "No little broth?" she wondered.

She spoke of my brother: "As sensible
as he is wise. You weren't here
for his suicide. But why
do you two still argue?" (Mother,
we've discussed this.) She spoke
of my sister: "Too young. Too short." Of me,
she said nothing, and coughed.

The drapes had been taken
to the detention home;
The piano had had to be put to sleep.
I took the funicular
to the attic: a last look at Father
with his red snapper eyes.
As he had always wished, I got the blear off
the pinball machine. Downstairs,
the windows were hissing.

THE HOUSE

"Next time," I suggested,
"we could just get tickets to the laundromat."
"It won't be long now," she disagreed, straightening
her wimple. "Almost nothing
is left of the floor. Sit down
and listen. The house is selling."

1910

"When you're drunk it's so much fun"
young Anna Akhmatova wrote
to young Amadeo
Modigliani in Paris, where she honeymooned
with her first husband, Gumilev, also a poet,
who had introduced them:
                        She stayed and Modigliani
made sketches of her,
sixteen drawings of Anna in the nude.

"When you're drunk . . . your stories
don't make sense. An early fall has strung
the elms with yellow flags." A Russian woman
having some fun. She visited Paris again.
And there was café life in Petersburg,
at The Stray Dog.

When the Revolution came, her husband
was arrested and shot. She put this into poems.
Her son Lev Nikolaevich was imprisoned
for ten years. Then eight more years.
She would visit the prison ground
waiting for hours to hear news of him.
It felt she was wafted
in the courtyards, like the leaves.

1910

It was a threadbare life, sometimes
near starvation. She went on writing.
There were other husbands, she was threatened
by the authorities, she was praised
by Stalin. Six feet tall, described always
as queenly, her effect on men, magnetic.

Anna chose her writing name on the belief
she was of the royal bloodline
of Ghenghis Khan. Life was blessed
and it was turning. She felt
herself clairvoyant, her hopes
of freedom, white birds flying
against the black sky.

But she would not go to live in Paris,
or anywhere in the West, where she could have stayed
in comfort. She wrote, "I am not with those
who abandoned their land." But some believed
it was to be near her son that she stayed.

When he was released Lev Nikolaevich
was bitter. He felt she should have done more.
He wrote, "You always sent
the smallest packages."

One of Modigliani's sketches
always hung above her sofa
in whatever room she occupied
during her unsettled life.

ACROSS AMERICA

Well-known Burger Chain Adds Crickets to Milk Shakes

How Police Found and Shot Remaining NY Prison Escapee

'Testicle-eating' fish from Amazon found in U.S. Lake

Dead Whale Washes Up on East Coast

Pope coming to United States: Where and When

Starve a Fever, Feed a Cold? Really?

ISIS Beheads Female Civilians for First Time in Syria

Movie Star Walrus Dead at 21

Consumer Reports Finds Some New Cars Burn Too Much Oil

LONG HOT SUMMER IN NEWPORT

When they did not have a great deal to say
to each other, they reread their correspondence, fairly
quietly, in separate rooms of the rambling house.
In contrast to what had occurred
in Cremona, these days were the occasion of a reliable
pretext, a series of formal events, exhaustive
refurbishings, a grail hunt for the perfect
robins-eggshell blue. She would go without an escort
half-asleep at daybreak. For the next hour
his voice was all that could be heard
in the sleeping house. Then he stripped himself
of rank and feeling, in the rehearsed concerns

of noon, or walked to the nearby stream over the blanket
of decayed leaves. Their friend's last words had been followed
by a month and a half of silence, which opened
new possibilities. No one had considered dying
in an anteroom of unconsciousness. And where
did that put you, since we can only imagine
in body terms. "Later" became the nickname
of some hovering uncertainty.

LONG HOT SUMMER IN NEWPORT

        But we met
at the church with cameras and children. The stale air
of the nave shuffled their secrets, dealt back
this new hand; for which everyone is grateful,
we say. The little quad was planted
with acanthus. The shared music of early youth
rings in memory, but nothing else is like this
disease that the brain ate. The shined-up cars
and the sobriety were prominent, for this improvised
siesta their lives had become. Is it true we have lost
our ancient urge to tell each other our stories?
The gloom held them fast, almost
tenderly now.

ECHO

The thing I wanted, thing
I prayed for,

It is green
it has a name.

The thing that found me
in the park

wandering
with my camera, walking with my spade.

It is late
it will go into the dark.

GIACOMIN'S BIGGEST 0

Jim Neilson was in the penalty box
For holding Don Kozak and the Kings'
Power play was swarming
Around *Giacomin*, crouching low
In front of the cage to protect his 1-0 lead

—who started the season by surrendering
        19 goals and losing 3 of his first
        4 games—
Bob Berry

Fired
A bullet from the slot   *Giacomin* kicked it
Out to his left
Dropping to the ice
Sliding to his right
Leaving the left side of the cage
WIDE OPEN

"It's a great honor to be known as the top goalie
        in Ranger history," *Giacomin* was saying
        softly into the microphone in his dressing
        room.—

Juda Widing was there at the left side 10 ft
Away without a Ranger near him   he shot
Knee-high off the ice
Toward the unprotected net

Without a Ranger near him

GIACOMIN'S BIGGEST 0

Somehow *Giacomin* flung
Back toward the goal, stuck up
His left-hand catching glove
And STOPPED THE SHOT.
For an instant the *Ranger goaltender* lay sprawled
On his back in front
Of the goal cage, believing
The puck was in the net.

"Then I raised my head,
looked down, and saw it there
by my arm," he said with a sigh of relief.

Let's hear it for *fast Eddie,*
       Whose 3-0 shutout was the 41st perfect game
       Of his career. —

"I don't recall doing anything
different. You have to be a little lucky
to get a shutout.
You approach every game
Thinking 'shutout,' but of course
You don't always get
A shutout."

—"You have to be a little lucky
to get a shutout.
You approach every game
Thinking 'shutout,' but of course
You don't always get
A shutout."

—"You have to be a little lucky

RIGHT ALONG

—Allegro non troppo

Now the party is moving
Into a final-like stage
You can feel it move
Like the night
That lives in the ocean
The plash of little faces
That move from the clouds
To the rolling water
A couple of new
How-de-do's, ok?, just
At the moment you're balancing
On one foot to imitate
A long-lost crane,
Just a second, I'm leaving, ok?
& I want to tell you
Life is
A rather large sheep dog
With your face.

ONE OF A KIND

The active fat fish

                                            The big trout tailing near the rock

In a faraway land

                                            In a land none of us can hope to see

We are moving closer to each other

                                            We are approaching another unfamiliar land

I want you to hurry up

                                            I shall always be too slow for you

Thank god, & then the wind
    strikes up through the grass

                                            Everywhere small creatures are amazed

All of your flesh, throw away
    & forever

                                            Save only the broken shells of the eggs

ONE OF A KIND

The dune buggy is just a provisional
    threat

                The real danger is not on the
                sand

On the other hand, there is music

                There are songs we are not
                permitted to hear

Here & now, that is what always
    is so very cosy

                The secret, the forbidden, the
                active fat fish

The fattening splash of laughter

                The sopping calories of
                dreams

Sadly, my dreams are losing their
    memories

                Mine are intolerantly real

It doesn't matter, we can sneak
    away

                There is no safe country
                anywhere

ONE OF A KIND

Too bad about all the rocks in the
    ocean

                Too bad about the sharp
                    coral reefs

Actually, sharp cutting edges can be
    endearingly familiar, & personal

                I am in love with blood

I have reconsidered my position

                This has only increased my
                affection for suffering

Hyacinths always infuriated you

                Even lilacs rob me of my
                sleep

Locked in the dark room of the ocean

                Nothing visibly moves

The entire idea covers us with awe

                We have no wish to be
                uncovered again

ONE OF A KIND

Only a little something to hold close
    to our mouths

        Nourishing as bread

It's a good idea to suddenly fly away

        It is glorious to discover
        wings

Then the baby got up from the floor
    to speak

        Found he had not learned to
        stand

This is more happiness than you
    can expect

        He bellowed from the floor

Your first smile was more welcoming

        If I smile again will you smile
        back

Hello, A well-done piece
    of sarabande

        A treat for the eye, the mouth
        & the hand

ONE OF A KIND

I just want you to say "All right."

All right

*One
Of a kind*

www.ingramcontent.com/pod-product-compliance
Lightning Source LLC
Chambersburg PA
CBHW050443010526
44118CB00013B/1655